*Nearer By Far*

**Also by this author:**
Signs of Australia (photography)
Domestic Hardcore (poetry)
Soft Riots (poetry)

# Nearer By Far

## Richard Kelly Tipping

**University of Queensland Press**

ST LUCIA • LONDON • NEW YORK

First published 1986 by University of Queensland Press
Box 42, St Lucia, Queensland, Australia

© Richard Kelly Tipping 1986

This book is copyright. Apart from any fair dealing for the
purposes of private study, research, criticism or review, as
permitted under the Copyright Act, no part may be reproduced
by any process without written permission. Enquiries should
be made to the publisher.

Typeset by University of Queensland Press
Printed in Australia by Dominion Press—Hedges & Bell, Melbourne

Distributed in the UK and Europe by University of Queensland Press
Dunhams Lane, Letchworth, Herts. SG6 1LF England

Distributed in the USA and Canada by University of Queensland Press
250 Commercial Street, Manchester, NH 03101 USA

Published with the assistance of the Literature
Board of the Australia Council, the federal government's
art funding and advisory body.

**Cataloguing in Publication Data**

*National Library of Australia*

Tipping, Richard, 1949- .
 Nearer by far.

I. Title.

A821'.3

*British Library* (data available)

*Library of Congress*

Tipping, Richard.
 Nearer by far.

 "UQP poetry" – Jkt.

 I. Title.

PR9619.3.T5N4     1986      821      85-20287

ISBN 0 7022 1905 3

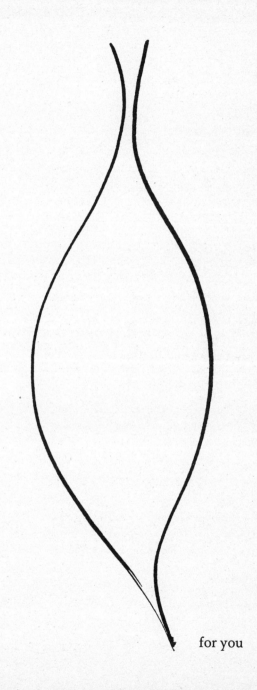

for you

# Contents

Acknowledgments  *xii*
Poem: Nearer By Far  *xiii*
Afterthought  *xv*

## THE POSTCARD LIFE

Untitled, 1974  *1*
Vipassana Meditation  *3*
Nowhere to Go, Nothing to Do  *3*
The Way One Thing Leads  *5*
A Little Unlicked  *5*
Hiking Down from Clouds Rest to Vernal Falls  *6*
The Sacramento Fair  *7*
The Bells of San Miguel  *7*
A Small Monkey  *8*
Train Steps, Java  *9*
Malay in Three Weeks  *10*
Tehran, November '77  *11*
New Surrealand  *12*
Bali  *14*

## THE DOLE BLUDGE AT CUMQUAT LAGOON

A Shoebox Full of Grasshoppers  *19*
Dr Hunter Wants His Money  *20*
The Desire for a Sneeze  *21*
What Have They Been Eating?  *22*
North Adelaide Parklands  *23*
Looking In  *24*
Poem in Search of Itself  *25*
False Alarm  *27*
Anyway  *28*

What Happens Then?    *29*
Maybe    *30*
Vytas and the Satellites    *31*
Before We Go    *32*
Pelicans    *33*
Deviation Road    *33*
Women's Work    *34*
Just the Facts    *35*
Kicking Stones    *36*
Limitlessness at Ruby's Cafe    *37*


KICKS & KISSES

Fragments of 1971    *41*
Chalk    *42*
Always Now    *43*
Love & Freedom    *44*
The Simple Act    *45*
Forget It    *45*
Conversations around a Full Bed in the Dark    *46*
Hillside with Two Figures    *47*
Body Surfing    *48*
Lisa at 22 Complains    *49*
Living History    *50*
A Rare Treat    *51*
Humber Vogue    *52*
Turning    *54*
Heading North    *55*
New Holland    *56*
The Cafe Domestique    *57*
Cowra Street, Mile End    *58*
Blue Mountains    *60*
The Return of the Baby Monsters    *61*
Maze    *62*
Staying on Top of It    *63*
Listening    *64*

viii

## SIGNED, AUSTRALIA

Adelaide   *67*
The Coorong   *67*
Driving to the Mildura Sculpture
    Triennial 1978   *68*
Wilcannia   *69*
Casino   *69*
Byron Bay   *70*
The Road to Roma and the Bottletrees   *71*
For My Father Michael at Nambour   *72*
Near Toowoomba   *73*
Hanging Rock, Victoria   *73*
South Australian Journal   *74*
  Port Julia   *74*
  Rapid Bay   *74*
  Gliding Near Gawler   *75*
  Cape Jervis   *75*
  Hackney   *76*
  The Flinders Rangers   *77*
Mangrove Creek, NSW   *78*
Mangrove Creek Revisited   *80*
Friday — The Ridge   *81*
Bowerbird, The Artists' Camp   *82*


## NEARER BY FAR

Australia Pty Ltd   *87*
Them   *87*
Advertisement   *88*
The Minister of Enlightenment
    and Propaganda   *89*
Notes on a Cultural Invasion   *91*
See Australia First   *92*
Telex:Big Brother   *97*
Animal Liberation   *98*

War     *99*
1984     *99*
Fascist Cooking (A Recipe for Violence)     *100*
The Palace at Midnight     *101*

## BETWEEN THE LINES

On Photography     *105*
Just after Michael's Death, the Game of Pool     *107*
The New Tax Year     *109*
What Can You Say     *109*
Checklist for Starters     *110*
Off the Top     *112*
The View from the Roof     *114*
Nanao Sakaki on the Roof at Bondi     *115*
Coogee     *115*
Southern Crossing     *116*
The Ear of the Tree     *118*
Ben Buckler     *119*
The Clones     *120*

## LIVES OF THE POETS

Tender     *125*
Days of Our Lives     *126*
Chris Barnett at Art Unit     *127*
Don't Miss This One     *128*
Poet at Work     *129*
Train to Mount Macedon     *130*
Studio     *131*
Upon Making a Videotape of Les Murray in the
    Series "Writers Talking"     *132*
  The Body Language     *132*
  Even Paranoids Have Enemies     *132*
  Arguments with Time     *133*
  Literary Gang Warfare     *133*

Talking Forests in Chatswood    *134*
Getting There    *135*
At Some Ungodly Hour    *135*
Locations    *136*
Day 2, Driving through Sawmill Towns    *136*
Politics Sticks    *137*

# Acknowledgments

*Poet's Choice 1977, 1978, 1979; The Friendly Street Poetry Reader;* No. 2, No. 3 and No. 8 *Friendly Street; Dots Over Lines (Recent Poetry in South Australia); Poets Australia Catalogue; A Time to Choose (Anti-Nuclear Poems); Nation Review; Dharma; New Poetry; Get Out; Overland; Opinion; The Great Australian Whiting; Open Door Broadsheet;* the *Bulletin; Polar Bear; Compass; Post-Modern Writing; Aspect; Spleen; Mattoid; Fling!; True North/Down Under; Brave New Word; Street Poets Broadsheets;* the *Canberra Times;* the *Age;* the *Australian; Your Friendly Fascist; Kunapipi;* and to radio stations 2BL, 2JJJ, 2SER, 3RRR, 3CR, 5UV, 5MMM, and 5CL. Thanks to the organizers of live performances at the Nimrod Theatre; the Art Gallery of NSW; the University of Adelaide; the Adelaide Festival; the Sydney Festival; the University of New England; Powell Gallery; Roslyn Oxley Gallery; New Partz Cafe; the Cafe L'Absurd; the Montsalvat Poetry Festival; Friendly Street; as well as in Bern, Milan, Venice, New York, Berlin, Munich, London and elsewhere during 1984/85.

I am indebted to the Literature Board of the Australia Council for its generous support, through a General Writing Grant in 1981; and to Nigel Roberts, Martin Duwell and my mother Barbara Stewart for their comments on the selection of poems.

# Nearer By Far

WARNING! THESE POEMS ARE ADDICTIVE
AND MAY BITE, NAKED AS HIGHWAYS.
THEY ARE NOCTURNAL, POLYGAMOUS,
HUNT WITH SLOW KNIVES FOR FRUIT.

DANGER! THESE POEMS ARE SHARP
TONGUES THAT STICK INTO NOOKS
AND MAY LAUGH AT FLAT MOMENTS.
THEY STICK TOGETHER LIKE GUNS.

NOTICE! THESE POEMS AREN'T MODEST
HALF MOONS, THEY LIGHT UP AND
BURN WITH A BILLION DETAILS,
SPREADING PAPER AS THEY WALK.

LAST CHANCE! THESE POEMS ARE DIRTY
AS THE EARTH, AND AS RESILIENT.
THEY MAY CHANGE NOTHING, PROUD
AS A WATERFALL, BUT STAY ALIVE

TO VOICES IN THE THIRD NEW
MILLENIUM. PICTURES OF FEELINGS,
ANGRY AS BUTTERFLIES IN GLASS JARS.
BEWARE! AUSTRALIA, NEARER BY FAR.

# Afterthought

This book collects together a hundred poems written over ten years, chosen from the high pile of certified verbal artefacts resulting from my 24th to 34th years to heaven. Poetry is still a dirty word, assumed to be one kind of difficult speech, where in fact it is as various as music. The poems have grown from strongly fluctuating impulses between head and heart and voice, in a life of such diversity and intensity the memory still surprises me. Words become alive in their own speech can be precise to perception's feelings while treasuring the harmonics of ambiguity. Poems scrawled on envelopes, pinned to trees, carried in newsprint, sprayed onto urban walls, discovered like lighthouses between sheets of paper: poems asking to be left alone, to be read in the head, and others speaking out, wanting to be uttered, with the printed text the musical score. My hope is that this book can breathe as a whole body, and the poems can live as a society governed by isness and rightness, as a habitat containing wildly different creatures, with differing intentions and metabolic rates, various as people, not all of whom anyone can expect to like. If form is the atomic structure of content, then each to their own, free as nature within its laws. Punctuation varies: sometimes the extra speed and casualness of lowercase suits things better, and the "i" shouts less than "I", but these are the ongoing excitements of the King's English in a cheerfully anarchic republic working hard to invent itself. Think ahead — it wasn't raining when Noah built the Ark. Time goes by in great blasts. Choosing the poems was difficult, too many friends trying to hang on to the only liferaft. My great thanks and love to all those who've shared the road, and our sanctuaries, through these spinning nights.

*The Postcard Life*

# Untitled, 1974

                orderly trans-negatives then
persistent as the smell of crap
  lw / left behind by cuckolded cricketer
gone home to claim his wyfe

             what can you say about time
between the moments that you ask it
    to carry weight as a witness of your consummate
decay
       when even to be married

                   odd moments when
it was as if language just stoppp
e nah unnershtan

crazed solipses, the beserk eclipse
of passing one hand before the mirror

ssomewhere in west africa
you can have it all, astrologer, except licentiousness
of purpose intermixes politics

and you might do well to starve
meaning, searching beyond the explicit
for those fig pluckings
when the planet is starved

not qu
     ite

assured: even the layout is tedious
and the content

that should be visible in bulk
at a first reading, merely enticing

support of a few drunk friends
far removed from australia day

## Vipassana Meditation

Beyond the darkening tumble of pumpkin & corn
in the dilating pupil of evening,
a barn, with makeshift tapestries
for walls, sitting perfectly still.

Within, supremely cushioned, almost surrounded
by quietness, a cat begins to purr.
The walls breathe gently. Blue light
crackling from fingertips and toes.

## Nowhere to Go, Nothing to Do

Poised like an ampersand at dawn
balanced on hunger's nostril
counting breaths – anapana – how
do you ride a bicycle? The wandering mind.

                        This on the first day
And on the second:

Impermanence, impermanence,
the endless disappearing trick of time –
brushed from my fist, the wounded mosquito
tangling in a spiderweb & . . .

     *

Tingling, the body electric,
a marble imitation of an eyeball

glistening like just-licked fur
hovers above a silver disk of pain.

                      This on the third day
And on the fourth:

The skull is a golden cone atop
the body's tent, swept singing! with
skin-light . . . gone. The snooze
of flowering mint & a velvet cat's meow.

      *

Within the empty vessel of the head
the road to Reno aches far off, jets rip
the earth's blue belly right across,
scrawling words on mirror water.

                      This on the fifth day
And on the sixth:

The creek chattering in one ear.
The creek gurgling out the other.
Smooth & cold as a well-worn pebble
the mind awakens, dreaming of the sea.

      *

Relishing abstinence, sense desires peel off
like old love letters − but the endurance
of an idea to stay attentively put
here! exactly, is not so easy.

                  This on the seventh day
And on the eighth:

Pierced by starfire, i understand myself
least of all. The moon has lain
down with the yellow pine. Torch notes.
Fat-bellied ants rear up across the page.

4

# The Way One Things Leads

to another these days, nothing will fit
if we assume a place for it.

The way a sudden splash of red
geraniums, blustering in a fizzure
between pale wooden houses
reminds me of last winter at Glenelg
slicing fat tomatoes by the stove
just as Dolores Park appears (dogful
of mexican palms & stray conga drummers
announcing a new rhythm for the afternoon)
with a dark blue mailbox
parked over there like a child's mouth
dripping with blackberries, i push
a letter home in, inspired by you, curly-headed
roller-skating girl, whooping with delight
at everything moving, roar of tiny wheels
on concrete, spinning to a stand
stop! around a pole


# A Little Unlicked

& i am tender sirloin, bleeding in a tray
in the refrigerated window of time –
this happens, just as a streetcar
slicing my vision of 20th St in two
hands it back to me, being gone.
i cross over Mission & idle
drinking carrot juice in a corner store
handing the cup back, empty
but for a little unlicked froth

# Hiking Down from Clouds Rest to Vernal Falls

the last time an ice age
   scrunched through here
      i was still considering life
         as a proposition
between the sun & the moon
   to freeze our balls off
      for boulders, chill the womb
       chocablock
with tiny granite whales
   & call us a day — but history
      was warm, & taller than sunflowers
        the redwoods grew, & sugar pines
dropping seed bombs, it was green
   & breathing now, holding nothing
      back, the water falls
       & falls & will be falling

# The Sacramento Fair

for all the broken eagles
lying by the sides of roads

await the ghostly night sweepers.
but the toad —

choking smell of rubber
thoughtlessly is lifting them

like tattered kites
above the Sacramento Fair


# The Bells of San Miguel

Because there are so many stupid
things left in the world
the bells of San Miguel
go crazy, rang
wrong, a song for the tourists
eating pork chops in bright cafes,
the lovers by the waterworks,
barrow-wheeling boys & all
the dogs in town complain at once

# A Small Monkey

We were silent in the dining car
of a zeppelin, cruising south southeast
over the Malacca Strait when

slap! we arrive as two people
aboard the Taipoosek, steaming to Singapore.

We've been here before. Standing on the bow –
come and look! – you see the same
dark dolphins playing tag; the bunch

of green crabs outside the kitchen
helplessly alive; the fruit merchant, on holidays
with his children, involves us

over supper, talking about chinese food
in the old days: a small monkey
held seated in a metal frame

with a head fitting, open at the top
so the skull can be cut around
and lifted off, the brains then

warm, in a natural cup.
Nobody feels like a biscuit
but – remarkable! All this is new.

The whole ship humming in the night
we lie down with ourselves in a cabin
suckling far out at sea.

# Train Steps, Java

the night sounds fast –
a black cup shattering

vacant stretches
when the mind disappears

in a place you might have been
yourself

an eye of god
modelled by particulars

the hand no less of god
than the most astonishing

machinery yet devised
in the nineteenth century.

the steps are hard.
the buddha-grass tastes hot & sweet

# Malay in Three Weeks
(found poem)

Lesson Seven.
Examine the following passage
and repeat each sentence in Malay:

What time is it?
Eight o'clock.
What time is dinner?
(At) half past seven.
Please come at a quarter past six.
Shall I come at six o'clock in the morning
or six o'clock in the evening?
What time is it?
I don't know.
There's a clock in that room.
Today we're having pork for dinner.
We eat meat every day.
I go to work every morning.
I drink tea every afternoon.
It's already four o'clock.
I must go out.

# Tehran, November '77

All the children ran
to see the Empress of Iran

blowing out the candles
on the carved ice swan.

Soldiers the colour of cracked mud,
taller than poplars

the palace wall
imprisons the Holy Forest.

# New Surrealand

twice discovered
intended paradise

the islands lie
like torn postage stamps
in far flung oceania

sheep scattered like valium
on a bowling green morning
just eat and wait

little old english cars, parked
like cherished grandmothers

on the mown shore
of cold lake taupo
feeding the sparrows scrap
roast take-away chicken
mourning the maori wars

here, where the ageing waikato chief
te wherowhero was chosen

colour television
certainly improved cricket

kiwi fruit, hand spun wool
crumpled white paper snow

umbrella-wrecking weather, wellington
boots, the routes of change

sheep farmer non-abstractions
agricultural thinking
the politics of the average
man on the street, an ordinary bloke
saying o jesus, piggy muldoon
by the short and curlies
is easy, but bloody smart
tactics to get your head punched
in christ's church

# Bali

The spaceport is standard &
after customary sifting procedures
transparent reality tubes fan out across the island
on the turtle's back, take you to your precise level.

Kuta Beach, Ubud
or something more detached?

Nobody wants to be identified as Typical Tourist
    grabbing experience, sight seeing
        through instamatic eyes

down a bamboo lane, a maze, to smoke-dark huts
two sea turtles, hands tied together
punctured bamboo string
eyes wet & dark & clear

later, returning, one lies in a bellyflop
    on a hard low block, dark neck blood pouring
        into an old plastic bucket

        the other turtle, already dismantled
            thoroughly washed
                grades of edibility arranged
head intact
            the clear dark eyes, the head
        above a burst of flesh delicate as a red anemone
            as you watch
                    mouth stretch
      open in a yawn &
              turns half over to
                    look

                straight into you
     alive,  alive
     a minute more
                    holy
                         satays for the wedding
         a time to praise
     the near dead,
                    the way of things
                              & be glad

# The Dole Bludge
## at Cumquat Lagoon

# A Shoebox Full of Grasshoppers

Therell be plenty of good images to flick through when im dying. Coming up over the morphett st bridge past fowlers lion factory; the low dry growl of a paradise bus going past the maid & magpie; vacant afternoons wandering the length of adelaide arcade, and back again. adders. adelady. laid. i used to want to make up a molecular model of the people around whod laid got laid by or slept with each other. molecular beds. no correspondence will be entered into. danny meets julie and its a wow. julie recently un-married paul whos just started living with paula. paula used to be with danny, and danny used to be with paula, tho only kind of. she had a room at boffa st when ramona & franky were there, and that got a little weird. ramona finally disappeared again to melbourne when frank split with barbara. pity. dave moved in and paula shifted back to her old place at glenelg, where ace & co were set up. ace is interesting because he connects with rhonda, violet and possum as well as julie, and rhonda is linked to dave, keith, danny & jim, who lived with possum off & on for nearly a year. barbara & star. dave & barbara. o, i forgot mary. barbara & mary. theres a rumour about ramona & geof-frey, but thats ancient history. geoffreys still with whats-hername. julie mated ace, wally & jerk last year, apart from her thing with keith. wally says its getting a little tight and walks off the set. says its easy for you to be blase blase, youre hardened like old cheese. goes away mutter-ing to violet about retrospective jealousies, sexual pedigrees and little punches to the heart. i asked jerk what he thought about adelaide. its like living in a shoebox full of grasshoppers, he said.

# Dr Hunter Wants His Money

Recently i dont write letters anymore, its too exhausting. as if any good would come of spilling the beans: went there, did that, thought about something else but i forget what. love always. the days go past like cars up & down the parade, one after the other though some go faster, traffic light to traffic light. id like to know who does the timing, especially a few hours before dawn when youre homing along at a cruising speed and the little bugger way up ahead goes green yellow red. take off the foot and let her glide in slowly, hoping to be in second when the word is go, but no. you snap on the immobiliser and stop completely. utter stillness. in a foreign country you could make use of this time to look around but here its like always. tap your fingers on the steering-wheel, glance left glance right and make a flying start. lights coming up fast behind, you know the rest; or maybe this time nobody notices or cares particularly as usual and youre already fast asleep in a comfy bed. the days go past and still i dont get any letters. perhaps thats because you dont write any. o very smart. what if i told you i once wrote thirty two letters to a woman i loved and the only address she gave was "greece" – did she ever send me a solitary kind of word? well, yes, but thats different. this is six days straight i didn't get any letters! last week i got a dismal little note for mrs a. fox who apparently used to live here. if youre reading this, mrs fox, dr hunter wants his money

# The Desire for A Sneeze

Theyre playing silly-buggers downstairs. i can hear somebody knocking but thats a long way off. thered be wind in the trees all down the parade about a month ago. the rubber plant trembles. it took a serious group of the council boys one week to give the whole lot the yearly karate chop. operation arborphobia. how the chainsaws curse! why are you cutting them? ah they mess up the streets, the wires — that ones higher than the flats! by tuesday theres a brass plaque nailed to a tree: "in wintertime the tidy equalize what sproutings we have done as english trees for english birds o green force. all power to the powerline." what did garrie say? all power to the noble lie. bill says it doesnt matter where you are as long as you know what you are doing, which was good. somebody cranky is putting the milkbottles out next door like the postman at talbot lane — used to pull up on his red bicycle, lean over the front basket, dig his hands in & blow on the whistle until one of us came out, then go for the letters like a hungry child in a bathful of jellybeans. apparently it was a dadaist act and we were the target as well as the circle of criticism. we never asked him in. cold coffee. where are all those fabled poets, thumbs in ammunition belts, leaning back in the deepest corners of forgotten bars? if people arent buying theres no stopping them, but so what. no trees, no leaves, just regulated trunks with the stumps of sawnoff arms starting to bud. affection for all things living sweeps over me like the desire for a sneeze.

# What Have They Been Eating?

The backyard is casual, like an old tennis hat almost covered in seaweed. a loopy breeze is shooking the silver gum when i step out to see Pearl, the cagey old sulphur-crested cockatoo, sounds like pouring Woodies lemonade over a transistor radio. the dark precision of dog turds bleaching in the sun; two broken bottles and a disarray of empties heaped by the back fence; gravel loosely strewn; Pearl on top of the busted van, squarky, cockatooish, doing special variations called rhapsody in a small place defined by wires. demolishes the cuttlefish i brought her like a hungry footballer with a packet of crisps. outside of a dog a book is mans best friend. thats because inside a dog its too dark to read. remember that? old friends show up and talk themselves into coffee. quiet days in the kitchen while the percolator perks, till the three dogs burst in, silly as bushrangers in a supermarket. daves dog henry lawson sits aloof and stockstill by his chair. whydontchatakemtothe-DOGclub, dave says, extracting a crumpled yellow pamphlet from his ethnic bag: read that! "Train your dog to be a well-mannered, appreciated and accepted member of the community. To walk quietly at your side. To sit quietly while being patted. To behave in the company of other dogs. To come promptly when called. To obey commands immediately." its a pity that isnt an obedience MAN club, says susie, the sweet little bitch. whew! randy! shiva! what have they been eating? if you havent paid by now, mrs fox, youd better. the backyard hasnt moved: casual as a young baritone at the moment before he lowers his plump cheeks into the bath and begins to sing.

# North Adelaide Parklands

you slide on both heels up through the park.
the evening is unpolished brass.

this city, saint vincents gulf
sucking through a single plug.

onion grass, indeterminate as seaweed
slickers on the spaceshoes.

you find the place you landed
but theyve left.

the long grass whirld
in a clockwise departure pad —

horse-fresh & delicate
dung steaming at the centre

with a timid heat.
its a sweet relief after the sun

goes out to meet the stars.
finally a shadow larger than night

is standing next to you,
and begins to eat.

## Looking in

two years in any face
marks change.

what do i face?
    my "lines in the mirror"
            predictable as the crinkle-cut
    chips in a take-away basket
neatening their structure
                into thought

no images beyond the language's
intractable domain

# Poem in Search of Itself

after alls been said & done
in intricate necklaces of words
you have no central idea, no force
larger than yourself to direct you
away from the desk saying this is not a poem
i hate poems about the poem
it must be direct exploration
using the facilities of words like
the last line has been thrown
youll have to swim it alone − no discovery
there but a pleasure in pure statement
bordering on the descriptive, so what you see
must be other, the other side of surfaces'
other cheek, whatever else is inherent
in the emotion event as signpost or point
even this square of speckled carpet would
tell you everything if you knew how to look
without trying to lose yourself, immerse
yourself equally repulsive as lovely, no
pleasure there − searching around for a foot-
hold, for a starter to fire the gun, for an
acrobat to fall into the afternoon papers
for the cars parked outside along the street
to shut all their doors at once, turn on the
lights and let us watch their batteries fade
as the moon "comes out from behind the clouds"
is typical longwindedness, no direct
exactly getting there, getting the poem along
its own path winding between ideas and
(ideas in sounds! seated in the brain of the tooth,
the foot lungs) that body of feelings we inhabit.
distance is no space. time only matters

when we're stuck in it.  impenetrable interpreters
– nothing as it is –
as if you could be present in each thing's
continuous coming into being
regardless of "meaning" – but meaning
that you're not really needed for the huge flip
of the whale's tail outside the museum
sending the shoppers like a shower of mammal flowers
through the bright spring air . . .

## False Alarm

i never wrote that letter
to Gafir Abrahim, who left
an address and asked me to

send him a publishable photo
of the wall on the Anzac Highway
with A REVOLUTION IS COMING

lettered up big & red
(he'd already written the poem) because
by the time i got down there

the wall was smashed straight through
and all you could see was
the smart-arsed face of the new

Le Cornu Furniture Showrooms

# Anyway

he doesnt call me boy
anymore.

the laundry is up the road
loaded with laps.

around the oval they put
BEER IS BEAUT

and he was loaded
stank of fun

giving me the inside
theories of what he felt

burning the shirt
leaving the iron on.

i want to be a young wife!
but he comes home cold.

# What Happens Then?

My grandmother is growing
smaller; not that old
quick look, but a kindness
at the bottom of a letter
rubs her eyes.

She smoothes
the stiff sheet's folded edge
like a child's hair.
"Soul, *my* soul", she says, then
"only half an hour left in this."

Her skin is wrinkled finely like the sea
photographed from a distant planet
on a clear, crisp day
with a good wind blowing.
"What happens then?"

She turns away
        from the sealed window
with both eyes closed. "I don't know —
half an hour's a lifetime", then
"nearly time to go"

# Maybe

Boiling chopped sheep hearts
to feed this dog cheaply –
    too long since we last ate meat
    to stand the smell, the fan
    with four slow propellors
    my grandfather's last wish that summer
    clearing the way –
let them cool in the bathroom, with the african violet
and light's slow suffusion through frosted glass
the afternoon rain
                dampening the Anzac march . . .

till the hearts go cool and hard
outside under the leaf-dropping vines
and Maybe comes up, starts chewing one.

she ceases eating, looks up –
why are you standing here?

Dear dog: so you want to be human, well
you can't – the nose and the ears
give you away, to guarding.

Sleeps in a curl
against my belly, utility lover.

# Vytas and The Satellites

satellites land on sundays
on the far side of the hill.

it must be the setting
invites their soft descent

into the blackberries
where they glow, eloquent

as rotting pears. vytas
brings a cool one back

across the valley, chuffing
in gumboots &

makes it the base for a barbeque
but no one needs meat

## Before We Go

we are walking, my sister
ahead by three years, and me

zooming slowly
(slightly above ground but

still apparently touching it)
down the rutted puddle track

until the secret place she knows
where no dream is abandoned

by decay: rotting buses!
fiery trucks with burnisht trays!

we climb in through the window
of a cadillac, remembering to turn

the ignition, engage reverse and
check for redback spiders before we go

## Pelicans

space is curving in with time
towards the light.

earth is everywhere
seeming to eat us

like the city eats the river
brings the local into view:

pelicans on a weekend off


## Deviation Road

it happens every time
i end up here again
late 70s milieu
eternal saturday afternoon
come, the sky is burning
this river must flow up

# Women's Work

discovering something
you were never introduced to –

digging fencepost holes
wiring it up

the handicap race of "you can't do it" –
out in the wild bush for days
the opportunity of handling things

among the insensibility
of bullock-breaking men

to be Mary, Joe and Julie
driving tractors, rounding the cattle
fixing bores

# Just The Facts

Well, Officer, after we shared a strong bong
the whole room felt like sherry

kinda sweet, kinda dry –
"i just couldn't sleep

from wanting you inside of me"
on a pro-skateboard

cruising gently around the porch –
we were burning the candle at both ends

and not a little ripped
when in she wanders, the nocturnal itinerant

with Josh on the piano, tickling the ivories
at 4am, in a cottage on the cliffs

at Owl Bay – but that's all another story.
the phone starts to breathe

and largens, swelling on its hook.
animals made people:

never forget that. the Earth was helpless
against sheer will and a good idea.

Cosmologies entwined: so Eternity IS in Love
with the productions of Time!

now you know everything.

# Kicking Stones

Brainweight keeps me aground –
the gravity of observing, browclutching.

Cartoon image: me holding you by one foot
floating off into the vast dark subject.

You're so furry! I'd like us to be a pair of Taipans
wrapped around each other, a tangle of rubber bands
or two sperm whales, don't they come
leaping out of the ocean, bang huge bellies &
collapse, their love so huge?

"I'll have the sorest cunt in Adelaide!"

but by now the poem is twisting away
a skyrocket with a certain bent

A story full of facts and fancies, a compost heap
sprung with the stench of the new

# Limitlessness at Ruby's Cafe

we live in the mind
ahead of time

past that is always
escaping us

at ruby's cafe
there are thousands of poets
running on a single spot
within the brain.

the brain includes the foot
and goes strolling:

thought that feeds on itself –

the smell of old people frying eggs –

one word on the brain's bright surface
pushing another off –

within the moment's
avalanche

the only way to hold the moment
would be to die in it –

we're living like tommy ruffs
nibbling when we dine, pulled out of music
on a single taut line. don't get ahead.

even a few years in this situation is
instantaneous in archaeological time.

swirling ancient memory fabric
dust on an empty road

how can such a safe life
be so precarious?

and how solitary to forget

*Kicks & Kisses*

# Fragments of 1971

cottaged alone
at winterdark

we cannot undo
the selves we wear

our absolute
unsheddable skins

crusted, bruised
with accumulated self

catpaw mist, tapdrip
& leaky nose too

details – all
trodden, worn
down with use

those old padded
dogchairs in the shed
smelling of bone
scraps & warmth

the mind resides
quickened on the skin

# Chalk

You are conspicuous and charming
like a mirror on the city's roof
lending us the Snowy Mountains.

There are skiers trapped for days
on the brink of your eyes, your smile
illuminates them.

When you make love the snowfields
are white cockatoos scrawking to take off
and circle you like a line of chalk.

## Always Now

your lover's boots
      have fallen over in the passage.

his china pipe, alfoil
tucked around the bowl
black from hashish
sleeps on the windowsill
by your bed.
the satin sheets a part of my
birthday present, the eiderdown
a part of his.

on deep white carpet
his japanese guitar
quiet like a record in its sleeve.

not jealous

## Love & Freedom

If we were to be sacred
all the rest was bulsh
of no interest
except at bedtime . . .

when we talk about others,
their bodies & what we've done
with them, we don't identify our nowselves
with our being then

because jealousy is trivial
you said, neurotic & insecure
it was only half an hour
between friends

and anyone who says they're happy
is just easily satisfied —
though as the man said: even the worst
fuck i ever had / wasn't too bad.

## The Simple Act

lying together
hemmed in        private silences
resentful, hardly forgiving
even the desire
to sooth       love's surfaces
after anger

"i feel lonely too sometimes"

the simple act
     wiping the whole tape clean
         to turn
      & hold each other simply
without a word

## Forget It

You being you
with me, with me
being me with you

thinking about him
thinking about you
with me

thinking about her
talking about us.

Forget it.

# Conversations around A Full Bed in The Dark

### 1

For a woman to
stay interested
the movie must go on
endlessly changing –
rhythmical: mystical

but men explode, sigh
like tired projectionists
while women love
their softest decline . . .

"at least men do finish –
calling that break –
oranges at quarter time!"

### 2

For a woman to
understand a man
is a kind of injury.

There is no opposite.

Do you understand me at all?
Of course, she said.

To get up in the cold
stubbing five toes on darkness
to write that

is typical.

# Hillside with Two Figures

Mornings without which
sleep. Wet lashes of grass,
black-eyed daisies
folded like old beach umbrellas –
in an abandoned paddock, falling away
through unsharpened fences, the fireplace
and the sheep-run
a monument to unnoticed effort.
The apples are crimped
and fallen, all coddlemoth and bruise.
Pale buttocks of folding
hillside and gorge a white bird swoops up
in a pendulum
                  whoop of song
the licked-clean slope,
tiny fluorescence of flowers
stark thistle and thorn –
the goldtops still asleep
in their deep and foggy roots
there are worlds within the world – creek moss
floating islands
a struggling ant would sink –
birds smaller than butterflies
invisible humming wings
that carry us up to a hillside
where you hold me
like a tree hugging rock

# Body Surfing

The inside history of our times
not touching, distant as Japan.
My expectations filled a truck.
You were the Girl on Her Stallion —
i lay by the creek and smoked
tearing up love's telegrams
letting the grass grow over me
like a month.  Strange tastes
called "MISSING YOU" and "XXX" —
image replay, dream video
dissolving personality spacesuits
eyes gleaming stones in a creek
hair sprouting from rocks
hands that wave from the tips of branches
wildflower ears, a beard of bees.
The wide screen flaps
tossing the whole love movie's cast
out into the cheering Drive-In.
My parent's marriage was like this —
hearts in mouths and shaking knees.
Brave hope, brave lunacy.
Suddenly you Return from Overseas
strolling through shuttering pigeons
silk dress swirling over me
saying it didn't really happen and
don't look back.  It's just what i need!
You're a surfer yourself and appreciate
how off right off can be.
With my brother's optimistic shout
ringing in my ears
to charge across the open beach and crash
into the unexpecting waves.

## Lisa at 22 Complains

about men
asking so hard a woman's
hard put to refuse
that specialness:

"what's good is
having a few close friends
who don't get addicted to
your hips, if you can
keep yourself on top
of the predictable desires
for a security blanket . . .

who ARE you? i've yet to
fall in love"
    she says
this
very slowly, a hand's length
from you lips

# Living History

transparent as newspaper
take the basic facts —
you can't.
tragedy's not brittle, subtle?
breaking apart is a part of things
like the way beaches keep moving
and Countdown keeps getting more boring
the more you look at sound
pumping up the rubber floats
of feeling against sinking
into words that can't survive
being written —
so much for the rock
and so much for the stone —
love it as you might, you're stuck
living history, alive and alone

## A Rare Treat

You were always rolling
the ultimate
little number, as a rare treat
to stretch things out
all the better
to love you with,
more skin on fire, more red wind
through your hair and toes
to be twinkling
blue light —
far inside, far away
waiting for the future, now
sweeping us both
into the Way

# Humber Vogue

dusk drive from Orbost – wet & spooky –
first night we slept far end of beach track
shhshh – um of rolling surf
                    wind in our circle of trees
letting warmth commingle with candleflame
      our sighs
         lifting into morning's promises . . .

sliced cling peaches
honey poured from a jar
our skin fresh grass –
the just mown smell

second night we slept by roaring sea cliffs
the tent flaps clapping like a crowd

    "once a woman starts to give –
    once that whole is open –
    it's very hard for her to stop
    no matter where it leads her"

        southeastern south australia
        steer and pines
        volcanoes worn down like old teeth

mouth watering speculations:
lobsters or crayfish?
completely out of season
we eat the tinned sardines

        a mauve rose grew
        a child's clenched fist

disrobed
duck winter lake
jonquils huddled in a bunch
our raw wool blanket, seats lain back
    wild birds calling
drumming rain on a warm car roof

# Turning

### 1

Being inside you means driving
with the horn on full blast
blowing a bald front tyre and rolling
through the safety rail straight over the edge

### 2

loving for days'
slow motion
our shirts crisp ripple
in a tight upturning breeze

### 3

deepening delight, four open eyes
beneath the surfaces      skin clings to
a thumbnail moon, spiralling galaxies
– our bodies' hum

### 4

not even the wind
has such tiny fingers

# Heading North

i love you more than a tree full of frogs or
a bursting creek, because you hear loud ants
the scrape of shaving and the sea
making love with rocks.

you leave rainforests where you walk —
parrots and pythons, intricate orchids
slipping from your freckled shoulders
like embroidered gowns.

you don't stop when it stops.
i'm axle to your wheel: careering magpies,
mottled doves, quick flapping away
from the first car for hours

# New Holland

i love you like raining refrigerators
when all our Christmas's come at once
and Australia is getting hotter by the minute
you are the missing quantum leap
shooting us into inner space
where loving is strictly thermonuclear
and foreverness is instantly real:
we're pulsating in, imploding stars
that make your flushed cheeks sparkle
like the Supreme Goddess as the Void
tonguetied on your kisses
so impeccably random, sublimely empirical
you must be a sister to Duchamp
rediscovering the black hole in Art
and WHERE CAN WE GO from there but HERE
where you're free to be anything
Holland is a long, long way from home

# The Cafe Domestique

*for Christopher Timms*

the energies
> of wiping
>> the table
>>> down
> clearing off all the
mess
> is instant
>> & continual
in the cafe domestique
>> abiding
> half-love for
dirty dishes
>> spontaneous arrangmenets
> of the eaten
>> enjoyed
>>> is the eternal
swab
> of cleaners    cleaning
is
> you:me
>> leaving nothing
but sparkl
> ing beginnings        for
>> new
>> conversations −
still life with
tea towel
> forever    repolishing
the implements
>> of thought
meal's moments
>> carried past context
> into anecdote

57

# Cowra Street, Mile End

Mild endless Spring —
hands & knees all Saturday
in what'll be the vegetable garden
(weed-choked square of rented soil)

The dark alluvial of the Adelaide Plains
built upon, divided into private lots
& lawns needing water
in the driest state of the driest country on earth

The Italian owners (no fence
next door) keep half a flock of pigeons
locked in a dark metal coop
breeding to be eaten in "our" backyard

& their killer alsatian, nose wet
glowering at our gardening, blaming us
for the bullet last week
(buggered his back leg) will dig up
our herbs again

leaving only the strawberry
frog's squeaky call
like wet fingers rubbed on a tight balloon

Lisa, Mama, bringing bowls of fresh pasta
sauce that takes days to make (minutes
to eat!):
>            "sevena keeds alaready, Guiseppe
>                    i tell im
>                            mya bones are tired
>                GETa young girl
>                            buta for me
>                    the house,
>                            the children . . . "

We live directly beneath the relentless descent
of towering soft jet liners, slow, fat,
magnificent, sedate, cutting like a chainsaw
through our rattling heads.

Luckily we don't mind.
Smile Endlessly.
Leave town
for good.

## Blue Mountains

David's house in autumn valley
rock path creek       goat chain
moss bath       baby gurgles
breasts among buttercups
"oh dear
              milk all over his face"
striped beetles
on leaning grassblades
slowly hitchhike copulate
                          bleet says goat
to lawnmower music far away
a roof-nailing easter sunday

twinkling spring water       the brimming jug

first stars
          for our two-month old friend
gazing wide-eyed
                    cross-creek, half-moon
clear chill air to the handspun shack
a slow log fire, grumbling bellies
to-be-whistling kettle, toasting bread

# The Return of The Baby Monsters

Structurally tired
The main desire is to sleep for 8 hours
Sure we sometimes get drunk
  like the Normals, not with fierce need
  but genuine desire to take flight
  as granted, & fly . . .

waking up    at 6.15
to gut-tugging hellos & calls
     only a parent knows
  as must:
     The Baby (per force)
comes joyously in
endlessly across your face
      (of course)
a bliss bomb
   splitting you into Day

# Maze

slide-sorter
placing, arranging
abstract intuiter
eyesight modifier
window opener
& eyes that fly out through it
open, photo seeds
scattering across a lightbox
in an attache case –
coastal parks
the ecosystems of arborphobia
you're living on the edge
walking the line –
it shows, these images teeter
brinks of view.
body structures – outlines
and corroborated form.
freeing the geometric gesture
to become story's signposts –
windblown pants, sheets &
nappies, documenting labour
celebrating placement –
the motherhood manuscript
in bodyprints & photos,
on the line.

## Staying on Top of It

what absurdity is this i've embraced
turning off the TV after another great expose
of the corruptions of the Queenslanders –
the rest is inedible like my blossoming overdraft

\*

saturday night, how to keep body & soul.
the permanent distractions.
clear strong flame of inner self.
a life as lived: too many million moments
to fit into a single poem – that spark,
spinal narrative, body language
whizzing into click-clack-clack
like the question of who / is going to do
the washing up / and who wipe up
the twinkling old plates and glasses:
three of us in two rooms
sounds too generous for the way it works:
a little squashed, a fraction overloaded
when you add the plants, hired TV, hired debts
what do we own except ourselves and books?
maze you'll understand – when i get up early
morning vague and you're nonstop specific –
the clouds still matter most
when we're on top of them

# Listening

### 1

Temptation's wild virtues
are eccentric, a circle's
eclectic draw —
succouring on cast-up
directions, the erection
can wait — sweet talk
gets you nowhere here
love's edge
being this hot, soft
slippery hard —
only language can elongate
so well, the lovers
stop, half-turn, smile,
listening.

### 2

Bridges made of song.
The instant's treachery
is vanishing —
only memories of barbeques
sunset across an arc of beach
and children banging music
pile all the secrets in
a pocket full of thorns
on pungent roses —
we're not tempted
only to sleep in
self's tossing barricades —
singing love
              don't come easy

*Signed, Australia*

# Adelaide

a sea so flat
you can skip
stones on it to the horizon

your heart
only survivor in the raft
reaching magic island

the moon so
close you sneeze
clattering plates


# The Coorong

*for Adrienne Sach*

st matthews passion, easter saturday
silversky sheen of cockleshell

the principal of the vertical
lain flat

divided by water
coloured by morning

a crackle of teatree sticks, potatoes
spitting butter in the foil

one fat flounder
struggling in a net

# Driving to The Mildura Sculpture Triennial 1978

*for John Stokes*

Empty Good Friday morning
backroad South Australian towns
washed out blues of living local sky
sandhills in the wheat paddocks

walking the irrigation pipe,
a little girl tapping with a stick —
roos and emus sleepy in the shade
of an empty fruit packing shed

swimming old man Murray's muddy flow
ducking the beeline attacks of flurex speedboats
& skiers out to pop out skulls . . . chest ache,
vowing not to . . . and what to . . . do
about said body . . .

the longest hot showers in unwritten history

Riverland Radio playing the Bee Gees Greatest Hits
15% above distortion level, three tents down

Huge full beacon moon
heading for a midnight eclipse

Australians don't mate, apparently.
The camping ground is so crowded and so
quiet after the fires go out.

# Wilcannia

The emu at Wilcannia
raised by the Barkanji
would pick damper out of the fire
chase dogs over the Darling River Bridge
hang around town;
old white local kicked emu in the rump
emu didn't notice; kicked again
emu turned and kicked
a gash straight down one leg.
next day emu's run over by a truck.


# Casino

a drawerful of obscure tools
for a dollar the lot.

a hereford in the butcher's window
carefully crafted in mincemeat & fat

# Byron Bay

On the corner of Wordsworth Street
thick stumps of the eucalypts
all that's left: professionally chopped
like blown safes, abandoned to rust.

Surfboards are the second biggest industry
after the slaughterhouse, after grass.

When the Royal Commission came around
they'd turn up in a big black american sedan
two guys with briefcases — set up the portable
electric typewriter and start asking questions.
Twenty minutes later: see ya!
People were leaving town.

On the ridge to Coopers Shoot, bamboo gone wild;
sharp rich grass, prime beef country —
a woven tropical matt for cattle fat —
few giant trees left, each standing like a city
playing bass chords to the wind.

Our hideaway shack's steep mudslick drive
with psychedelic spiders. The caretakers
are surfers, living a regular life:

> "smoke a bong at dawn an hit the surf
> till about 11. crash out. have another bong
> an check if the surf's up. pig out on dinner.
> more bongs. rage on till about 2. crash."

Easternmost point: each day
starts here.

# The Road to Roma and the Bottletrees

rock tumble slope
cattle & kangaroo

cattle  – lazy defiant, morose, roadblockers,
            heel-kicking calves
kangas – zig-zag bounds, whole families, curious,
            ears erect, sniffing

giant worn fists of stone
lichen covered, narrow-trunk white gums
land of spider waiting, traps
between smooth pink flanks of rocky hill
pissed on by parrots (fluorescent green-yellow-red)
goanna's funny fast-forward run
straight up a ringbarked river gum
        gripping tail        exact claws
        puffing speckled orange-black throat

slept in intense roll-over dreams
in a clinker-built dinghy with dad
samurai washing their hair
a paradise for absurd objects

# For My Father Michael at Nambour

we are miracles of the wounded heart
completely healed – welcome
to the exhausting present tense
overgrowths of stars
squash a mosquito and stare at it for ½ an hour
all night veteran psychotropic surfing movies
to halfwatch, waiting for the electric alarm
at 6.15 when dad comes wandering in
quite coughed velvet.
real time's faster than heat and more physical:
it takes years of days to relax – here's
the backroom of your soul – it's a hole.
are you waiting for perception to arrive
in the mail? (fail)
pulling over for wideangle photographs
the slanting stripes on trees, the gasp
of queenslandering seaside towns, juxtaposed
culture fantasies, the invasion from mars,
a lithe girl, naked, doing handstands in the pool
but there's no need to talk except
what's for breakfast? ginger biscuits and beer.
it's another non-day
says michael from the melting hammock

## Near Toowoomba

i want to write a painting about
sunflowers, their hoary heads
bent in prayer, a trembling square
of drying yellows pushing to
the limits of a field edged on all
sides by pasture where the glowing
browns of cattle moan and mow
the fattened shoots while from the
humming hives bees come to suck
the dying bloom and the sun
flowers crowd and seed


## Hanging Rock, Victoria

"Don't look at the trees:
        they might turn into snakes!"
Rocks, dry leather, cracked old smiles
        lines around the eyes –
    tunnels, clefts, to eerie silent paths
        between the lines
The eyes of stone, its lidding mosses –
        spells,
    faces of shadow, clean worn bone
        dog-eared bracken
Near as the moon – breeze shiver grasses
        footprints in the air

## South Australian Journal

*for Nicholas, my brother*

### Port Julia

flat slap of sand and oozing orange cliffs
vibrant as the barbeque on wheatfield's edge
with the farmhouse on holidays and six nurses
calling the shots: loin-lamb chops sizzling
under slabs of dripping-fresh pineapple
– a nip of rye, with rainwater –
kicking a soccerball high, in a paddock of onionweed
and soursobs . . . "Chase me!" . . . a child's strong cry:
the meaning of everything suddenly seen
as a Horwood & Bagshaw Harvester, greased, rusted
earth brown, waiting in the half-ripe wheat,
late winter.

### Rapid Bay

The beach is so wide you start to disappear
zooming across sand, the car eating land
like an ant on a banana cake, heading for the obvious
gaping cave, forcing you like a juicy tourist bus
into the only motel – into the earth-gut
twinge of piss and empty bottles, for the gypsum
shouting from the smokeblack walls . . .
They're mining alright, at the other end of the beach,
a whole poem away. The couple by their Range Rover
boiling a cuppa are right out of the ad: politics
as a progression of selfishness from stateless
to status and how come I've missed out?
Nick, you're incorrigible.

# Gliding near Gawler

Van Gogh would grasp this swirling sky
of colours on an empty canvas sown . . .
late afternoon's slow-kindling fires
awash with winter hues: orange, vermillion,
grey, pink, blue: the moment hugs you to it —
in air we live, in earth we will lie.

Lean blades of wing and cockpit's rotund eye —
the gliders pulling from green ground
till the cord is snapped, the tow plane dives
and all horizons vertical: overwhelming
silences, in the whack of air and rolling winds
that lift a human thought into lasting flight.


# Cape Jervis

We came from the winging ridge
that rollercoasts through flashing green
down in a gasp to blue —
land's end, the Southern Ocean's smashed
grey-blue and a horizon that bends
holding Kangaroo Island proudly, at a distance.
On a scarf and woolcoat day, the ferry wasn't.
Two pelicans on serious round rocks agreed.
The seagulls stayed optimistic, despite avocado.
Mysteries of seaweed, stone and shell
all beacons of substance in our child's eyes
the sponges were satellites: the tractors still
in a semicircle, hogging that little beach,
holding their boat trailers out like hands
for the fishermen of Backstairs Passage.

# Hackney

The mornings are corkscrew tight:
just-Spring in Adelaide
and all the flowers shouting —
almond, jasmine, wattle, nectarine.

Shocks of bright weed, over
thrown thrown with caterpillars, rich
Wanderers in brown fur coats —
streets spattered with petals

on parked cars, sun-split clouds
and still-leaking rooves, red wine
in hand-me-down houses —
the lions roaring from the zoo.

# The Flinders Ranges

the wild
hops, red
swathes
of desert mountain
flowers, mid-Spring
on gate-opening
backroads,
splooshing the ochre
Holden through
glass-clear creeks
to Chambers Gorge,
late raw sun
jumping across
river-soak shallows
rock water reeds
wide gully wall
aboriginal ancient
overpowering cliffs
seven skin-taut bone
shot corpses
grey kangaroo:
the heedless scrawking
of a hundred white cockatoos

# Mangrove Creek, NSW

*for Neil Taylor, Sue & Crystal*

### 1

Bare-breasted in stinging sun
(from wrap around verandahs
of the only house for hours –
a painter's piece of heaven)
to follow the creek's slow
yawning swerves
unwinding down a bark–
flake track of smoothskin eucalypts
naked, stepping from the clothes
around their ankles. The bush flies
flirt, loud-mouthed as Saturday.

### 2

Valley of nesting plovers cry
while whip-birds crack
the pheasant pigeons coo:coo:coo
and startled cows
the dogs send thumping
cross-swamp, wide-eyed;
the black snake rolls
red belly round, S–
curves through dung.
One bull's gone puff-eye blind
and thuds dread circles.

3

Dharug, the people, gone. A name.
Cliffs can't stop weeping.
The National park starts there
on the ridge, beyond the tucked-
away ruins of farmers,
the skeletal edges of cast-iron beds
grown through the gums.
The gravestones are losing their tongues
for palm trees and roses,
chimneys and cattle runs.
"You who come my grave to see
Prepare yourselves to follow me."

4

Our children sapling young
amaze the creek, such tight-
formed bodies, the water dragons
leap past logs — under a hot
blue sky, exuberance of wattle —
raucous tiny flowers
from fern-spring grass
the hillsides peak: Spring tips
on sombre green. A lone blue wren
tip-tails and goes. Make love
among mosquitoes; no one knows.

# Mangrove Creek Revisited

Wet Christmas — the frogs cheer.
Goanna, sniff-tongue, gripping a dark branch
in bellies of cloud:
all the little clues come home
with a proud yell — dogs yelp
the ducks into flight, a circle
of casual but formal energy —
the handwriting of each tree
layering blocks of pattern
as the van bumps, skids, splashes
us back. My drawings; your poems.

*

I wanted to read Japanese poetry
by the creek, time-sitting you, Kai,
with a long yellow rope across
shallow sandbar water, set up
haul, fish and splashing games
for one — me in the brimming shade
not called to crocodile rescue squad
by your bright-eyed shout
but relishing the bilateral spark
and so missed half of what
you did, too late. Time's repeatable
isn't it? Sorry, mate.

# Friday — The Ridge

Carried Kai alltheway up, through scratching,
tough rocks, Maze copping a splinter, antbite,
& Jedda, always in the way (panting old Blue
Pointer) with Jock the Labrador
and Henry the Red Setter panting, up and
past — "Yow-w" says Black Feather the lean
ball-pop tabby cat, came along too, right to
the lumpy ridge (sparkling ochre sandstones)
run by Banksia Men and Secret Places, Sacred
Flowers. Maze couldn't hack it, essentially, only
so much tolerance, but still did (complaining,
shouting) climb to the middle of Nowhere: to
look down on the slow sweep of valley floor,
swamp and riddles of shape and date. Climbed
down through a squadron of weeping "native
pines" and delicate unknown bushyness, deadly
little blackberry shoots infesting crevices
and nooks of moss, to the hand-deep creek, where
we all stripped off and lay, bushy-tailed and
vivid, in the cool, meandering water, Mangrove
Creek, so called.

# Bowerbird, The Artists' Camp

*for Tim Storrier*

1

i miss you in this river full of stars
as the moon starts banging branches
and kingfishers stir in the paperbarks
i'm restless as the earth is, still
in time's slow ways . . .
Tim yells from the fire's circle:
"i can smell goanna piss!"
and whacks on another song – gone.
Frank slices celery, brushed with salt
"an aperitif?" and smiles into flames –
a deck chair full of painter.
Stories of the punch-ups for Art,
the fists full of brain, rolling off
surface, colour, texture, shape –
did you walk into a bus? Today
Hal Porter's in critical, hit by a car
and Jack Newton chopped by a plane,
reported by radio, twelve hours ago;
a day full of conjunctions, flashes
extremely concentrated: we're making
what we make here, alone
somewhere on top of the world.

## 2

Walked for hours along the wide, white
sandy riverbed: spiky-headed pandanus palms,
tiny purple-mouthed yellow orchids bursting from
between the river stones; pools of striped fish
racing shadows. Climbed through suburbs of snake
track and spiderweb, tracked along
under the towering ancient ochre cliffs: weathered
metamorphics, dream fragments.
Arnhemland is a wilderness of silences
shattered
by black cockatoo, by bronzewing, by you
among burst-pod flowering gums, needle
spear grasses, flies that bite; all the stones
are rusting.          Listen.          Soak up
the inhabitedness
of this rare earth, this chance to feel
two thousand million years as a flash
of feathers, a bright exit.

*Nearer By Far*

## Australia Pty Ltd

Yes — in suburbia's fixed stare —
if not for you then for your children —

a house, a place to work
an expanding purpose
 — who's nationality?
 — is the family in splinters?
 — are you for or against
   controlling private enterprise?
 — you want another beer?

the fat back-pocket vote.
the unreadable suicide note.


## Them

they dont look forward to the long weekend.
their lovelife is shredded paper and caged birds.
they kiss like tyres on hot roads.
they hurt to look at but stare with blunt steel eyes.
they are they were they will they did they want.
they eat only animals and white bread. look up
just to check for mistakes in the movements of clouds.
they create massive unemployment pools and unsafe cars
and drive them. you know who i mean.
they are tight as a rusted monkeywrench.
they start wars for something to do on saturday.
and theyre heading this way

# Advertisement

These Queens of the Sea reach perfection
in the early "kitten" stage:
boiled and snap
              frozen
                    for their journey
from the Abrolhos Islands
                  of Western Australia's
                         Indian Ocean coast
1.5 kilos of succulent
              white flesh and
                    full rich flavour
FOUR choice young and juicy
                  Geraldton Rock Lobsters
YOURS!     airfreighted
                    by 9am
              to your home
              or office
Come on,
           salivate,
                  you rich old pricks
                  you bellied bags of worms
                  you beautiful, beautiful people

crunch a little gore and stuff the gobs
wobble your pouches boot the yobs

All for just $35
phone any day or telex
Bankcard welcome

# The Minister of Enlightenment and Propaganda

Joseph Goebbels, late of the late
Third Reich, unwanted father
of modern advertising, the violent
incandescence of your ambition
to be more than the last
son of a carpenter's catholic wife
in the textile town of Rheyndt
scorched your name across the altar of a school.
Star pupil always – careful with appearances,
scorning the illkempt – delighted to
fabricate bad information and
watch the mockers squirm.

By the end you owned three hundred suits.

Virtuoso of duplicity, master of self esteem,
cynical of Catholicism – but silent
for so long as silence could be used – saving
until later your quote: "the Mass is the most
tendentious rubbish ever to be inflicted
on the intelligence of man, but
mightily useful
in proving man's capacity for absorbing crap."

Frail, good looking, with a polio limp
you hinted was the mark of war, graduating
after eight universities (restless, curious
about divergences, dirt poor) from
Heidelburg, Dr Goebbels found politics
confusing, and slept around.

Diariser, womaniser, nihilist detached
with a surprisingly slovenly and burly friend
introducing the works of Herr Karl Marx
you swung straight right
in Munich, that debauched assassins' town,
your glee when — finding that a sentence
stuck: "the truth must always be adapted
to fit the need" — you knew you'd found
a friend in greed, Mein Kampf.

Five secretaries, four telephones, always a plane.
That vast campaign of inspiring lies.
Wordmonger. Tongue twister. Language's murderer.
Writers abhorred you — how unfortunate. You loved
to be adored. Strength through Joy. Death to Doubt.
Mimicing the lives of the everyday —
from the stomach to the brain, via the heart.
Building enthusiasm, the factories to be forging
that great idea, the standard fraud,
Volkswagen — "the people's car" —
ha ha. Kinder, Kirche, Küche für die Frauen.
For the women: children, church, the kitchen
and the Jews the rats the jews . . .
no more.

Faithful to the last, your family beside you,
Berlin aflame, ordering an obliging officer:
"Shoot straight!"

# Notes on a Cultural Invasion

we're being invaded by cultural imperialist
thugs like ronald mcdonald & the marlboro man.
there's no more passive anti-venom, no more
sitting back taking it all in quietly. let's
blow a few logos apart & whack the bastards.
declare image war. go inner-ground insisting
on image integrity and outsmart the smart-
arsed telly-meddling brain tinkerers, the
product-feeling merchandisers, the slogan-
makers, the corpulant half-brained valueless
supermarketers, the monoculturalists, the
odds-on-suckers'll-buy-it sellers, the
media men, the military merchandisers, the baby
poisoners, the profit-mongers of power and
the people who make this crap and pay for it
to be fed into domestic systems of our eyes
ears brains guts and livingrooms. useless
competition. pseudo choices. all needing us
to agree to identify to borrow to buy.
messages of hope do get across: dry gumleaves
spinning in an eddy; the wild sky above the
cricket ground; bird tracks on a crowded beach;
a two year old boy kissing live red flowers.

# See Australia First

Let's assume for a moment that we're not near the end
of life as we know it — that
wide-scale nuclear
war
won't happen

that
the human population won't explode too totally
and there'll be enough food
no disastrous diseases
insects eruptions earthquakes droughts
no superpoisonous pollution
or mercury-wrecked seas
that the jets won't bugger up the stratosphere
letting the cosmic rays do a microwave
on us
that the newspapers will always
arrive
thunking on the concrete lawns

\* \* \*

if you have to climb a ladder
to see over the garden wall
tell us what you can see —
not how you climbed the ladder

\* \* \*

If poets are the early warning system
we need a nuclear vocabulary – explosive imagery
perception measured in kilotons, radioactive verbs
intercontinental ballistic meanings, stockpiling poems
the balance of mirrors, roads made of bandages
that lead to the heart of matter equals energy
and it only took one gram to blow Hiroshima –
thinking at the speed of light
the narrative spine resists shockwaves,
straightens for the fight . . .

\* \* \*


See Australia first, very soon.

China shakes with realization.
America is a drunk ex-boxer
cursing and punching in the dark.

Russia confiscates the moon
and harpoons Japan –
the Middle East reacts – a total oil ban
stopping Europe in its tracks.

Australia, nearer by far.

We're sitting around doing sweet f.a.
hoping no one remembers us and attacks –

dreamtime detached.

\* \* \*

Pine Gap – what's in a name? North West Cape
is a name. So's Pan Continental Uranium
and Omega. Nurrungar. Trident. Polaris. Pershing.
Nato. Warsaw. Cruise. SS20. Pact. Treaty.
Threat. Trigger.

Australia, you are a word.

* * *

This is a message from the United States of Australia:

* * *

America  stop bad-mouthing the struggle for freedom.
         can you believe the Indians don't want to
         nestle missiles in marlboro country?
         stop saying US and THEM.

America  you're a truck skidding on thin ice
America  a bald eagle with a hairpiece
America  the warning lights are flashing
         CREDIT OVERLOAD
         Central America is burning
America  the 24 hour factories
America  the itchy trigger fingers
         what is the meaning of the doughnut's hole?

         Mr President, your sincerity
         is breathtaking – are you plastic?
         the first presidential TV clone?
         you are so bland you are pentrating
                              these very walls!
         i just love your platinum lung:
                        how SPOOKY!

The Dead Watch Shift from midnight to 4am
at Pine Gap Spy Base, Central Australia, the boys
from Central Casting dozing at the glowing controls . . .
INSERT TEST RED ALERT . . .
the computer JAMS with excitement, on TOTAL

       Mr President, you had all the remorse you needed
       in advance? let us pray? i can't believe you —
       you did it? you pressed the Darth Vardar button?

WHOOSH! WHAMMO! WHAP! they're firing back! —
there goes Detroit — and the swap is Leningrad?
Come on, New York, stop everything!
You can't? Hello . . . Hello? . . . Hello? . . .

               * * *

America  what would you do without alcohol, sugar
           and nicotine? drink blood?
America  your flag is burning
America  Nicaragua El Salvador Lebanon Palestine
           Chile Angola Grenada Vietnam
America  the Russians don't know Afghanistan, either
America  the poor are getting poorer while the dollar soars
America  go home. Russia, go home.
America  true genius is yours — you break into tears
           at the drop of a hat and always come out
           with a profit . . .
America  we love you we hate you
           put your poets on the screen primetime
           and watch your ratings soar.

       have i said enough?
       do you want to listen anymore?

America  Miles Davis is typical of your brilliance:
          roll your tripping syllables and
          batter me with jazz . . .

Come back, America         to the future you promised
come back                  to your vision
                           of freedom for everyone
and deliver us from evil
now and forever
for thine is the kingdom
the power and the glory
for sure, for sure
fat chance, tough luck
we can't all score
but don't say the poor deserved it anyway
when half the world's your garden.

America i'm coming to see you.
America i hope you'll still be there.
i'll phone when i've arrived.

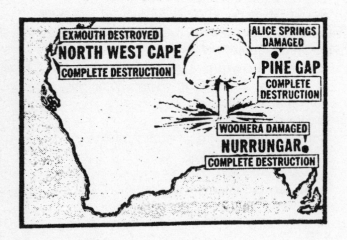

# Telex: Big Brother

NEWSPEAK LINGUA FRANCA DONTCHA HEY GOD
PEOPLE PAY FOR PLEASURE YOURE ONLY AS GOOD
AS YOUR PRODUCT STOP BEYOND THE DICTATOR-
SHIP OF THE ORDINARY IS THE WILL TO DREAM
STOP VIVA CUBA STOP COCA-COLA GO HOME OR
HAVE YOU GROWN SO DEEP IN THE JELLY HEARTS
OF NOMEN THEY THINK YOU ARE THEMSELVES STOP
DOES THINKING OF APOCALYPSE IN STRATEGIC
BALANCE CONTRIBUTE DASH WAKE IN FRIGHT TO
TEN STARVING CHILDREN FALLING OUT OF THE
FRIDGE QUESTION MARK THE TV SET ON FIRE
HAVING REACHED THE EDGE OF RECORDED TIME
YOU CANT ABOLISH HISTORY NOW THE NOOSE IS
TIED IN THIS GUT WRENCHING FEAR OF NUCLEAR
STOP STOP STOP ARE WE ALL MAD OR IS THIS
REALLY HEAVEN AND HELL COMMA IMPOSSIBLE
LIES THAT ARE TRUE BELIEVE ME I HATE YOU
AND EVERYTHING YOU DO SAY AND STAND FOR
MAKES ME SICK I WILL EAT GRASS AND CURSE
YOUR FOREVER AFFECTIONATE ENEMY BIG BROTHER
OVER AND OUT PAUSE DEAFENING THUD PAUSE
EXCLAMATION MARK SPACE SPACE SPACE APPLAUSE

# Animal Liberation

every day night day in flourescent laboratories
they are probing
the complex repeatable back brains of swallows
with thin long knives –
feeding fourteen selected poisons to piebald mice
watching the muscular reflex of the gut reaction of rats
with computer eyes
squeezing fresh hand lotions into the tearducts
of guinea pigs, cutting
the splintered cancers from monkeys
infecting the trembling future with abstract chemicals
for what?
"for money, mad man"

# War

The idealists are being booed off the stage again.
The people want to hear the cynics and the cynics
want war. After this one there's no before.
The war needs people but the people aren't quite convinced
they want the war. A compromise at last:
send the idealists to fight!

# 1984

The brilliance of the recent past
swept under fear

The newspapers are sniffing war —
after this one, there's no before

It's self-consuming and brags of power
the ideologies of fate

Shouts: "It's never too late!"
and keeps preparing, hammering out the vows

and promises that curse
disarmament conferences preceeding arms

Build it up! Stop that! Who goes there?
The trigger-fingers flexing

and practicing, bunkers full of screens
radiating maps and mathematics

as though life depended upon it
which it now does

# Fascist Cooking (A Recipe For Violence)

SHARPEN YOUR BLADE. ADJUST THE GAS.
BREAK A DOZEN EGGS AND BEAT THEM TO A YELLOW PULP.
GUT THE FISH. CHOP THOSE KIDNEYS – REALLY FINE.
SHRED THE CHEESE, SLICE THE BEANS
SCALD THE MILK AND WHIP THE CREAM – NICE AND THICK.
PEEL THE POTATOES, BOIL AND MASH. CRUSH THE GARLIC.
GRIND THE PEPPER. SQUEEZE THAT LEMON DRY.
THE OVEN IS NOW BLOODY HOT AND YOU'RE SIZZLING.
ENJOY AS YOU DESTROY. OUT OF THE FRYINGPAN
SOMETHING DELICIOUS
SLOUCHES TOWARDS BETHLEHEM TO BE BORN.
BON APPETIT!

# The Palace at Midnight

The Queen is bleeding tonight.
Full moon. High tide.
A great idea is born.

She unlocks the gates of the erotic
and Mona Lisa licks her lips.
OK. The Royal Family sweat

for their gold. Pass me that Crown.
Bring in the Tiger Butter.
Butler! Are the Princes' bottoms warm?

Where's the Women's Weekly? Thorns!

Tell His Highness to get in here.
Quick – beat me! Don't just kneel –
No. We can't wave anymore
you scabrous twit. Moisten the aching tips
of those missiles in the Bear Pit.

To sleep, perchance to dream!

*Between The Lines*

# On Photography

*for Robert McFarlane*

Veils' and illusions'
reverie.  She has dreamed
herself here
>for the photograph
>to take itself

like an actor is, a sparkler,
illuminating souls.

the literal and the transcendental
working together –

the quality of daring
amplifying the decisive moment

swelling light
the window changing as you move.

the constant ability
to be surprised –

just watching
the discovered forms

light: tonality: frame

to reveal and amplify
the breaking of even space

selection: observation: isolation

the juxtaposition of wonder —
the rainbow in black & white.

you don't expose pictures
you expose yourself

# Just after Michael's Death, the Game of Pool

The hot thumb.
That was so plucking subtle:
"I'd just like to accept things
and go for the general good"

Another triple-flutterblast rocks the room.

My father should never
have had children – could have been
a great pathologist – explorer
mapping the mysterious landscapes
of the skin – afterthoughts of body, thin
lines "distinction" into the latin names, not
having to worry so much about
Mrs Gatchilliano's chillblains, the kids'
runny noses, the cancer
already embedded in sunburnt skin –

The universe is at your feet, Paul.
"I'm just going to put it down that hole"

As history is a language map
thrown backwards

your absence is so fresh
it weaves a gap

My heart hurt too –

you wanted to be with us,
playing drunk pool till 6am

only centimetres from the funeral
pulling you away
in a tremendous gleam.

writing on electrons, entering
the body of the immortals

a shadow of the actual
midnight on the dot, in heaven

living by luck alone
the same things will still exist

we'd gladly be gods
but it would spoil the game.

so death doesn't suit you.
i'm sorry.

sore eyes, sore heart,
so praise the spirit that embarks.

try on these shoes – they fit – you move –
accepting the shadow of original clouds,

all that's tangible
is that you're gone, though the spirit is all
that prevails, this stops you're dead.

## The New Tax Year

i just kicked a cockroach
to death, very briefly
for entering my place
while pissing –
you know the feeling
guilt
damaging your shoe
kicking the wall
without a thought


## What Can You Say

what can you say
after that amount of wine
and valuable metal
traded across time –

unless the temporary perspective
wins as it should,
declares NOW an eternal premium
and fucks off for good

# Checklist for Starters

What YOU need to GET THERE, advises Lesley Walford, interviewed over breakfast by The Australian:

Ready?

* Rapidity of thought
* Lucidity of mind

* Quickly assess situations
* Be genuinely helpful

* Charm
* Wit

* Personal appeal
* Good looks (variable)

* Manners
* Money (but not too much)

* Talent
* Originality

* Art or superbusiness are best
  for crossing all social lines

* Depth and consideration
* Always acknowledge invitations

* The right flair
* Panache

* Drive (which implies energy)
* Confidence

* Determination
* Discrimination: some people might be amusing but

they won't help you get ANYWHERE.

# Off The Top

God i love you i hate you –
you threw me into this unbelievable mess
hardly a clue
the heroics of being ordinary
brilliance & all the pulsating stars
space dust on eyeballs at Bondi
no way out but in
straggling the quantum on last bus
home to self as family
the beauty, rage, heaven, pain
together again, so now matters
beyond a party's chatter and booze
more than infinity's bright eyes
and all the total of Saturday nights
(fresh beer exploding on the pavement)
Do you feel this conversation being watched?
It's true, nothing lasts
so does nothing matter
or something, calling, hissing, begging
drag blank matter into form
and love the leaping afterthought
that cancels all the future's debts
in a clear glass moment? Nein.
We're rubbing shoulders with time
and smiling "I understand!"
as if death was repeatable
as if another sentence automatically began
as if pure life itself was heroism
which is true, but relative –
the drama and the panorama and
the terrible stop. stop. stop.
Don't TALK about it, such

expectation of poetry
and the wretched pride of names –
you think this is a verbal game –
as if tragedy was somehow distant
and blessed by cameras
as if family life was a brand name
and the statistics of consumers –
as if holding your head above water
was a precondition of art
necessarily made of struggle:
so silence is golden and boring.
all the readymade words pile in
on an earth that keeps splitting
hairline fractures
through your mouth.
no excuses.

# The View from The Roof

*for Roland Robinson*

by compass point:

       sewerage works & flaming chimney
       manicured golfcourse
       faultline cliffs – picket fences
       tumble huge rocks
       jewfish fishermen
       yachts trawlers tankers subs
       sheer drop to crashing spray
       hard blocks of flats
       top of the Sydney Harbour Bridge
       & Centrepoint Tower's glare
       Bondi Pavilion
       blonde serve of beach
       bald green headlands stretching away
       Waverley Cemetery jutting
       (Lawson & Kendall there)
       Pacific blue waves, silver gulls
       probing helicopters
       black dot board-wait surfers
       chorus of biplanes roaring through
       humped ridges, littered with rooves
       offices apartments hotels
       the Aboriginal rock carvings on the cleared hill

## Nanao Sakaki on the Roof at Bondi

gazing at the city
from the edge
of the sea
he said

"just one question —
what are all these people
doing here?"

## Coogee

this was the outer edge
        of where you were driven
                coast-hugging, scrub-ridden

i know next to nothing
        my son sleeps in an aluminium pusher
                over your remembered bones

while i'm sitting watching glass knives turn to stone
        not guilt, indirect, but in tranquillity
                a gnawing edge, always

transferring in to where i conceive i am
        tumble-down flamboyant ribbed sandstone cliffs
                edging in verandahs of rock

with bright-boot fishermen
        throwing out long tight lines
                into rich-dark effluent enriched ocean

## Southern Crossing

all creatures are aware. intense existences
    the crumbling rock escapes
   ideas of time
         & change
  being aware of being aware
                  4 billion people
      full of stars –
         a single cell
  has planets and suns –
      all life emitting light
    into interstellar dreaming
with godness beyond us and swirling inside
  our days are full of all our days
               mor(t)ality
    a whole species run wild
going forth to multiply
        trying to alter
    everything
       generations of energy
  bleeding & building
        steering an unsteady course
      between excess
      and necessity
thrown into
life unasked
     stuck in said bodies
   a personal death
  half remembered birth &
love that doesn't feed upon
        returns

the fertilising eye
altering everything to scale
steps smaller than babyfeet
desire its own rules
"in the beginning was the word
and the word was WHY"
invigorating abstract thought, tumbling
through cycles of song, climbing
and unclimbing
the worn old mountains of poetry
four thousand million humans –
and everyone right
from their own point of view

scintillating ant-mound cities
forests full of starry frightened eyes

around and around
the wide earth turns –
a sleepy dancer

## The Ear of the Tree

In this quite ordinary infinity
(present forever, yet-to-be past)
the future is limitless.

Words are a thief's key
the doors of perception are opening to
the eternal instant (now).

What can saying say
but singing does? The radio waves.
The answer questions.

Time isn't action. We know that
thoughts are acting.
This truth's a blind man's mirror:

last night is still last night.
For a moment something precious will be
opening, and shuts.

# Ben Buckler

Pre-dawn pushes the darkness
inland, a roll of silence
banging drums of waves
pushing onto sandstone cliffs
a row a sudden pigeons
flecked metal hues
Sun punching a wedge
through sea, a shower of gold —
horizon the camel's eye —
dawn's old head
from thrown-open windows
handfuls of wheat
the eager pecking

# The Clones

i want my bunch
my family of self
in instant duplicate –
i want lunch
eaten by the clone who
shops, cooks, eats,
washes up –
i want the crunch of rent
and the bills all
handled, earned and paid
for by the clone for business –
i want a male secretary
with word processor
to type up, file, send out
poems, ideas and fight
the image war –
i want a clone to be
lover to my love, pure dad
to my child, being three
being another world –
i want a clone, curled
around a book fulltime
who feeds straight to
the swirling core of mind –
i need someone of me
watching nothing but movies
another for music, art, dance, TV
cross-cultural, a life
time's work just to catch up!
i plead for the hedonist
in me to be cloned
and soak up all there is to sense

while the spirit resounds
purely for pleasure –
yes, i want the clone
for conscience, to purify
and petrify morality –
i don't want to live
forever, i just want
nine or ten of me
NOW, one of whom is
always sleeping

*Lives Of The Poets*

# Tender

The Common Wealth of Australia

Invites tenders for the construction of a new
POWERHOUSE OF POETRY.

Specifications include:

A split-level tongue twister
For left and right hemispheres
Eloquent, passionate, ambiguous
Tough as nails, gentle as brail
With death-defying optimism
Key under each door, four open walls
Brute economies of compression & compassion
Generating wisdom beyond knowledge
Truth a necessity in relativity
Go forth into all the corners of the word —
Imagination is power.

Further details available from:

The Secretary of Inspiration
Department of Verbal Arts
Uluru Transplant Building
Sydney

# Days of Our Lives

Shelton's sleeping on the trampoline
Eric's asking the whereabouts of Cooper's Ale
Geoffrey's on the Montsalvat hairy cowbell
Bill's on guard against bushfires (literally)
Billy and Neil were last heard of
west of Alice Springs getting bush tucker
– a lot of friends are trapped in anthologies,
labelled and dated – but
Gig's playing the slowest guitar in local history
Michael's found the Lord and disappeared
Bob's retired with another Hawkesbury Grant and
a fine woman, fishing mythically
John's digesting images with an automatic blender
John Two's burying ash idiomatically
Laurie's dug in, assaulting the obvious
Pie-O's permanent director of the Anarchist Archive
Kris has started his own poets' post office
Garrie's kicking the advertising habit
Ken's bolted the door open for the sake of art
Nigel's got divorced again, just before the marriage
Rae's still working for professional unemployment
Sorry if i left you out

\* \* \*

for Shelton Lea, Eric Beach, Geoffrey Eggleston, billbeard,
Billy Marshall Stoneking, Neil Murray, Gig Ryan, Michael
Driscoll, Robert Adamson, John Tranter, John Forbes,
Laurie Duggan, Π.O., Kris Hemensley, Garrie
Hutchinson, Ken Bolton, Nigel Roberts, and Rae
Desmond Jones.

# Chris Barnett at Art Unit

suicide cheesecake

relentless pans across dachau, culloden
the battle of the coral sea, hiroshima
B52s saturation bombing bamboo

on the brink
of the bottomless
pit

you jump
into the firing squad

you martyr
to monologue

our life becomes
skulls, vomit
permanent tragedy
death and hell
pondered with a medieval eye

in the last days of the world
why abandon ship

# Don't Miss This One

Typewriter broadcast – sitting above the thump
of the real present – music – sifting explosive
stories of the past: Ivan Durant's portrait of
Bjelke, swallowing the blue jugful & producing
the (it turned out later) new realist penis to
– with energetic well-practiced plashing strokes –
draw a surprisingly good likeness of the Premier
in blue piss on the white papered floor; or the
schoolkids from Wollongong, visited the Yellowhouse
in '70 or '71 to probe the artists' co-op with
demands for right of performance: charging a full
theatre a clean two dollars each and opening
the fullwall front house doors – audience expectant –
suddenly facing the pedestrian traffic of
skinflick Kings Cross on a Saturay night –
true theatre – bringing us back to the booming
bass thump from downstairs here at Art Unit
where the Orchestra of Skin and Bones are playing.
We depart to catch it all before it's gone.

# Poet at Work

*for Nigel Roberts*

After the second book
words are a luxury, for a while
it's floorboards, walls & windows first
fixing up the house. Earth holds
wood before paper: measuring, sanding, hammering
nails into a near-perfect join
collaborating craft and art into a livingspace
like a typewriter needs table
& bum somewhere to sit, like you write
where you love eat and shit – it's all this crude
& this much work doing everything yourself
with friends who'd rather language
was the beam and skirting board
than actually helping build a bedroom in the real
world of "all this for a thousand dollars
and my holidays" – Nigel, you're so *practical*:
construct a new book, against the grain.

# Train to Mount Macedon

*for Ken Taylor*

Ah the whole annoyance, relentless
flat summer wheat, hard ground
you bastards — our bread
smells of blood, the train's long cry
a boring, horn-goring history,
the linear push to Diggers Rest — a stop.
Prune the gums like that,
they'll always suicide: say sorry
for your murderous
simplicity, your land-
clearing afterthoughts,
your pine planting at Clarkefield
and then Riddells Creek — a land
fenced flat and dumped as
Pastoral, the past is all.
Locked. Complete.

While Kai, 3, says
WATCH me! Watch ME!
Climbing up and over
seats, racks, windows
YOU DIDN'T SEE
WATCH DIS! I SHOW
YOU SOMETHING . . .
WATCH ME!
WANTA SEE ONE MORE?
DID YOU SEE DAT??!
ONE MORE!
YOU-CAN'T-GET-ME, YOU-CAN'T-GET-ME
TRY AND GET ME NOW!
SEE, YOU CAN'T . . .
WHY AREN'T YOU
TALKING TO ME!?

# Studio

The studio life.
Woke in early afternoon
to a backfiring truck,
shaved, walked two blocks to mid-city
to phone, post, newspaper, coffee
and back to work – endless
multidirectional and unpaid.
No dinner, missed the time,
ate bowls of raw muesli
till 6am, dawn being announced
by a light-flashing copter
crossing Pyrmont Bay, watch it
across eight lanes of freeway
busy making money.

# Upon Making a Videotape of Les Murray, in the Series "Writers Talking"

### 1   The Body Language

You have grown largely with your body of ideas
self evident, impossibly becoming flesh
as words dance, remeeting themselves in air
thanking the poem, page to mouth to mouth
to ear, resplendent, in solid soiled Les Murray.

On the tongue is a windfall farm, just around the corner
of a library shelf, anywhere: a mind's black print
on white abstracted pages, the luminous human earth
summoning its nightmares' and daydream horses'
sharp joy renewed suffering breathing, daring to speak.

There is a meter to the foot, out pacing ground
in the study of a writer's literature, who sings
the is-ful ah!-nesses of things . . . in iambic pentameter
the rocket will have to lie down with the lamb
and poets in free verse say: I utter, therefore I am.

### 2   Even Paranoids Have Enemies

Your enemies appear fragile, knowing by heart
hardened arteries and alcohol's eyeballs mapped by veins
they spin in the boiling water of their anger's heat
convinced of one hard boiled-egg fact: you're a red
necked liar, a papist stooge, a droog and

– worst – not worthy of the name of poet. Cough.
Robert Adamson, Michael Wilding should know better
but don't. They draw bright swords, pens dripping
and face bone-bare the crucial unextinguishable act
of it being 1am and the bottles all empty, shops closed,

the Muse having left. Nothing but saltwater to drink
unless abstractions would do it – or absinthe sucked, book
wise, from the aromatic armpits of Baudelaire: Rimbaud
still out there riding the tide to horizon's edge
where the sun flares up, curses, "Impossible!", and sets.

### 3   Arguments with Time

The argument against me was that I'd chosen Les Murray
because I could get the funding for him, and then
(I said) Bruce Beaver next. Roland Robinson was first
so it's fine company, I appreciate many poetries . . .
want to celebrate this way of seeing through saying:

a bite of the real works, poets compressed in live time
to electrons dancing in a box, a compounded articulating
of mind-body-spirit's demands, in words as given. Unquote.
This didn't go down well. Michael declared me bullshit,
I called him a pretentious prick, and that was it.

Debra had left, taking furniture and the kids, so
it's natural enough that Bob was upset, Nigel said, as we
veered the typewriter ribbon strip of Darling Street.
Was it Michael's car we accidentally scraped? O God
forgive us our trespasses, our disbelief, this deep sleep.

### 4   Literary Gang Warfare

This fight's gone on too long indefinitely postponed –
splitting the subtle ecologies of verse into rank
subdivisions of brick and lawn where no bird sings
and the sprinklers are on all summer. The Classicists versus
the Angry Penguins versus the Jindyworobaks – not done yet

in film, but another Great Unknown, the blue Divide
of our unresolved differences, city suburb bush and country town
vying with the Outback and the wrap-around Ocean's call
for our voices, ears and beer-quenched tongues:
to the unspoken intellects of race call and barbeque

the hunt is all conceptual ritual and the names of the fallen
a police matter, for the bail-out fund. God vs the Aliens
doesn't sum it up. Nor does Sex and Drugs and Rock & Roll.
All poets are equal, but some are more literal than others.
The obvious last line. Poetry is the politics of imagination.


### 5   Talking Forests in Chatswood

That rainswept Saturday I visited in early May, remember
the walls of books, the piles of toys, the range of children
from goggle-eyed two to book-locked eighteen: a pot of tea
for half the afternoon, topped with steam, tight lidded
in the age of electricity, we put on my video. Your beam

angled back across an emperor's couch was a smile
that counted: Valerie, too, never having met Roland, said
"I feel like I know him now". Your study is the one private room.
In a neatly crowded wooden house, I saw how the outcome and
income of your landed passion needs that half-silence

only city life and family life can give. You've built
a private crowd, my bloodline, domestic dominion
of all your resurrected past. Does this sound too plain?
I imagine the farm at Bunyah, the cow pads and paddocks
on paper, the daytrips to the bush for ghosts and flowers.

6   Getting There

With a fine crew of friends, loading the U-matics,
mikes, batteries, cords and lights into a hired bomb
we left the city's beehive hum, light-ridden
in cold half-dawn, the suburbs sleeping as we sped
against the thrust of trucked, indignant cattle.

A highway is a higher state of mind for an automatic
sucking on a full gut of fuel, the humming gizzards
of a Valiant Hemi 235 on full bore, getting there
the radio plays watered-down poetry, ads and news,
goes static — refinds the country, a new band, brewed.

Driving through sore small towns, waking to white bread
eggs and tea, a school bus pulls skidding to a stop
beside a 44-gallon mailbox and a gate, our road's black line
zooming through pocketed forest, the settled lands, flashing
fencepost to warning sign to words to views of the unbred.

7   At Some Ungodly Hour

Bunyah the fillet, the back-block, the elbow, delicate
as familial relations understood at the speed of milking
cattle walking, with accepting pleasure, to the place of suction
in a measured row. I like bovine lactic fluid too —
with tea, muesli, not coffee. Appreciate cheese. Milkers

translate to camels in a horizoned row, pyramids
cross-cut with shots of Pharoahs naked in museums.
My perspective can't stop late-night TV, the years
of wine, joints and movies; but that's a foreign language
here, your father ebullient with relished stories:

shooting three king parrots (glorious, common
as potatoes) potted for soup, brewed with herbs, tasted
and spat out, their meat tanging of stubbed cigars
after eating the wild tobacco. Or the black snake, hiding
in the back of the money-jar radio. Or the undulating uncles.


8  Locations

We started at the ruins of your childhood house
for "Cowyard Gates", "The Kiss of the Whip" and
"Midsummer Ice", with you plopped comfortably astride
a bald grey foundation post, looking into the sun
towards the five Scotch Pines your grandmother planted

and the ice-carrying hill behind, the buzzing
relentless draw of a Telecom dozer digging holes
– stops – releasing a silence split by the songs of birds:
"Both – that's the real country sound!" you said.
Got it all in three takes, packed and went

back to verandah you with Cecil, a father of oral history
for the vernacular tribe. A bottle of imported Scotch
for good measure, and traded stories, ignoring cameras –
a welcoming of space. Finally, after the roast and the rushes,
you sprawled, leisurely, "Homage to the Launching Place".


9  Day 2, Driving through Sawmill Towns

Too good a morning for roadshots, your Commodore taking
the Bunyah turn from the Bulladelah–Taree Highway
and pulling in a clean pan (cut!) to the inserted gate.
We were crew, and worked till a late lunch, filming
the typical run-down beauties of a sawmill town.

My four-years son planted raisins and almonds
already ant-dragged around the bulging eyes of potatoes
while we argued mid to wide shots under the ageing trees
for "The Broad Bean Sermon", a voice over dam and garden
with you calm as Sunday under the shadows of branches.

Then the long drive, perfect early Autumn weather,
to "The Gum Forest", and – grasping a sapling strong
as endeavour, your delivery of the casual idiom:
in short, what grows tall to be cut down, refreshing ground
for poetry, all that matters is difficult, profound.


## 10   Politics Sticks

My poetry, you wrote, rejecting a manuscript
was tangled in style, not dense enough, but that
is taste: equivalent to you pouring a giant pot of tea
1, 2, 3, 4 cups in a row, asking "Which do you want?"
"Three." Is thicker better by necessity?

My rhythm's personal, jazz folk rock reggae punk classical.
Teeth-meshed, brain-breatht, the abstractions
are just about genetic, and politics sticks – I mean this
sheet of paper imagined as a tree. To say we disagree
and to accept it. Leaves too much floating in the bloody air

suffocating our perennial anthologies. But so what
in eternity, if the planet is going to crash into the sun
does the enterprise matter? Yes. My home ground's rented,
a P.O. box my address, no place my own till welcome death
will let me seepingly forget the taste of bitterness.